Arizona
The Grand Canyon State

Marcia Amidon Lusted

PowerKiDS press™

New York

Published in 2010 by The Rosen Publishing Group, Inc.
29 East 21st Street, New York, NY 10010

First Edition

Editor: Nicole Pristash
Book Layout: Julio Gil
Book Design: Greg Tucker
Photo Researcher: Jessica Gerweck

Photo Credits: Cover, p. 11 © Momatiuk-Eastcott/Corbis; pp. 5, 7, 9, 22 (tree, flag, bird) Shutterstock.com; p. 13 © www.iStockphoto.com/Anton Foltin; p. 15 © Topic Photo Agency Inc./age fotostock; p. 17 Steve Bly/Getty Images; p. 19 © Charles O'Rear/Corbis; p. 22 (animal) Tom Walker/ Getty Images; p. 22 (flower) © www.iStockphoto.com/Loretta Hostettler; p. 22 (Cochise) Western History Collections, University of Oklahoma Libraries; p. 22 (César Chávez) Getty Images; p. 22 (Jordin Sparks) Kevin Winter/Getty Images.

Library of Congress Cataloging-in-Publication Data

Lusted, Marcia Amidon.
  Arizona : the Grand Canyon State / Marcia Amidon Lusted. — 1st ed.
      p. cm. — (Our amazing states)
  Includes index.
  ISBN 978-1-4358-9347-4 (library binding) — ISBN 978-1-4358-9788-5 (pbk.) —
ISBN 978-1-4358-9789-2 (6-pack)
  1. Arizona—Juvenile literature. I. Title.
  F811.3.L876 2010
  979.1—dc22

                                        2009026804

Manufactured in the United States of America

CPSIA Compliance Information: Batch #WW10PK: For Further Information contact Rosen Publishing, New York, New York at 1-800-237-9932

Contents

Welcome to Arizona

There is a state where you can see lizards and Native American sand paintings. In this state, you can walk on London Bridge without leaving the United States. In which state can you do all of this and more? The state is Arizona! Arizona is located in the southwestern part of the United States. It is east of California and Nevada and west of New Mexico. Utah lies to the north, and Mexico is south of the state.

Because of its warm **climate**, Arizona has one of the fastest-growing populations in the country. Arizona is known as the Grand Canyon State because it is home to the Grand Canyon, one of the natural wonders of the world.

The Painted Desert, shown here, is a popular place to visit in Arizona. This desert got its name from the colorful rocks that are in the area.

Cliff Dwellers and Cattle

People first lived in the area that is now Arizona around 20,000 years ago. Arizona's early **civilizations** built cliff **dwellings** high above the ground. Some of these dwellings can still be seen today.

In the 1500s, Spain sent explorers to the area from Mexico. Next came **missionaries** who wanted to bring **Christianity** to Native Americans. In 1821, Mexico became independent from Spain and later went to war with the United States. When the war ended in 1848, part of present-day Arizona became U.S. **territory**. Five years later, the rest of the area became part of the United States.

People then traveled to Arizona to mine, farm, and raise cattle. In 1912, Arizona became the forty-eighth state of the United States.

These cliff dwellings, in Canyon de Chelly National Monument, were built at least 700 years ago. They were built by a group of Native Americans called the Anasazi.

Dry Air and Desert

Arizona has an interesting climate. In the northern part of the state, the climate is warm most of the year. However, it gets cold in winter, and the mountains often have snow. The southern part of the state is often warm and dry. Very little rain falls there, and temperatures can reach more than 100° F (38° C) in summer!

Arizona has everything from deserts and rivers to mountains. The hot Sonoran Desert reaches north from Mexico up into southwestern Arizona. The Colorado River runs through the northern part of the state and then along the western border. In the Basin and Range area of southern Arizona, mountain ranges separate desert plains.

One of the lakes found in the Sonoran Desert is Bartlett Lake, shown here. Bartlett Lake is a popular place to go swimming and fishing.

A Truly Grand Canyon

Arizona's most famous natural feature is the Grand Canyon, in northern Arizona. The Grand Canyon was created over millions of years as the Colorado River cut through the rock. Today, the canyon is 1 mile (2 km) deep and up to 18 miles (29 km) wide!

The Grand Canyon has more than four million visitors each year. People from all over the world come to see the beautiful colors of the canyon walls and to hike trails around the rims. Not every person at the Grand Canyon is a visitor, though. A group of Havasupai Indians lives in part of the canyon. Their village can be reached only on foot, by mule, or by helicopter.

The Colorado River winds through the Grand Canyon, shown here, for 277 miles (446 km) before heading south to the Gulf of Mexico.

Life in Arizona

Even though Arizona is often hot and dry, animals and plants are plentiful there. The Gila monster and the iguana, which are types of lizards, live in the desert. Bighorn sheep and jackrabbits live there, too.

Many types of trees grow in the desert, such as the mesquite tree and the Joshua tree. Flowers, such as the reddish orange desert paintbrush and the off-white ghost flower, grow there, too.

Arizona's state flower is the flower of the saguaro cactus. Saguaro cacti can grow to be 60 feet (18 m) tall and live to be 200 years old. Other kinds of Arizona cacti include the organ pipe cactus and the prickly pear.

The white blossoms of the saguaro cactus open during cool nights. The blossoms then close by midday the next day when the weather is hot.

Farms and Factories

Because Arizona has so many beautiful things to see, more than 20 million people visit there each year. **Tourism** is very important to the state. Visitors need hotels in which to stay and restaurants in which to eat. Because of this, many people in Arizona work at these places.

Arizona has a lot of farms. Because the climate is warm, fruits and vegetables are grown there, even in the winter. Farmers also raise cattle, hogs, and chickens. Arizona also has many **minerals**, such as gold, silver, and **copper**, so mining is an important business there. Factories in Arizona make parts for helicopters and airplanes. Even parts of your television or computer may have been made in Arizona!

Here you can see farmers herding cattle on a ranch. Raising cattle is an important business in Arizona.

A Visit to Phoenix

Arizona's capital city is Phoenix, and it is located on the upper edge of the Sonoran Desert. Phoenix is the largest city in Arizona and the fifth-largest city in the United States. More than one and a half million people live there.

Phoenix is full of fun things to do. You can visit the Pioneer Arizona Living History Museum, which is a village that looks like a real 1800s town. You can see a rodeo or a Native American hoop-dancing contest. Other nearby places to see include Montezuma Castle National Monument, a 20-room cliff dwelling that is over 600 years old. Visitors can also see Phoenix's original capitol building. Opened in 1901, the building is now a museum.

There are many things to see and do at a rodeo. This boy is riding a sheep! This event is called mutton busting.

It Came from Space

In the northern Arizona desert, there is a large hole that is 1 mile (2 km) wide and 570 feet (174 m) deep. Rocks the size of small houses line the hole's rim. What is this hole? It is the Barringer **Meteorite** Crater!

Scientists believe that this huge crater was made about 50,000 years ago when a meteorite hit Earth. They believe that the meteorite was 150 feet (46 m) wide and weighed more than 300,000 tons (272,155 t). When it hit, it left chunks of iron scattered over a 10-mile (16 km) area. If you visit the meteorite crater, you can climb to a special area that looks over it. The museum there even has a piece of the meteorite!

The Barringer Meteorite Crater was named after scientist Daniel Barringer. Barringer was the first person to prove that a meteorite caused the crater.

Something for Everyone

Arizona is a great place to visit. You can see the **Petrified** Forest National Park, near Holbrook, where huge trees were petrified after being buried in **volcanic** ash millions of years ago. You can also visit Lake Havasu, in western Arizona, where the original London Bridge was rebuilt after it was moved from England. You can also visit a Navajo **reservation** and see sand paintings drawn on the floor of a **hogan**. You can also explore Arizona's beautiful landscape and enjoy the scenery.

Arizona's warm climate and clean air have brought people to the state for hundreds of years. No matter what you like to do, there are many things to enjoy in Arizona!

Glossary

Christianity (kris-chee-A-nih-tee) A faith based on the teachings of Jesus Christ and the Bible.

civilizations (sih-vih-lih-ZAY-shunz) Groups of people living in certain ways.

climate (KLY-mit) The kind of weather a certain area has.

copper (KO-per) A reddish brown metal that allows heat to pass through it easily.

dwellings (DWEL-ingz) Places people live.

hogan (HOH-gahn) A Navajo house made with logs and branches and covered with earth.

meteorite (MEE-tee-uh-ryt) A rock from outer space that reaches Earth's surface.

minerals (MIN-rulz) Natural elements that are not living things.

missionaries (MIH-shuh-ner-eez) People sent to other countries to tell people about certain faiths.

petrified (PEH-trih-fyd) Turned into stone after many years.

reservation (reh-zer-VAY-shun) An area of land set aside by the government for Native Americans to live on.

territory (TER-uh-tor-ee) Land that is controlled by a person or a group of people.

tourism (TUR-ih-zem) A business that deals with people who travel for pleasure.

volcanic (vol-KA-nik) Of or caused by a volcano.

Arizona State Symbols

State Tree
Palo Verde

State Animal
Ringtail

State Flag

State Bird
Cactus Wren

State Flower
Saguaro Cactus
Flower

State Seal

Famous People from Arizona

Cochise
(Around 1810–1874)
Born in AZ Area
Apache Leader

César Chávez
(1927–1993)
Born in Yuma, AZ
Labor Leader

Jordin Sparks
(1989–)
Born in Phoenix, AZ
Singer

22

Arizona State Map

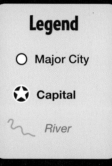

Lake Mead

Grand Canyon National Park

Colorado River

Little Colorado River

Navajo Reservation

Flagstaff ○

Lake Havasu

○ Prescott

Holbrook ○

Petrified Forest National Park

Colorado River

Salt River

Phoenix ✪

○ Globe

Sonoran Desert

○ Yuma

Gila River

○ Tucson

Legend

○ Major City

✪ Capital

〜 River

Arizona State Facts

Population: About 5,130,607

Area: 114,000 square miles (295,259 sq km)

Motto: "Ditat Deus" ("God Enriches")

Song: "Arizona March Song," words by Margaret Rowe Clifford, music by Maurice Blumenthal

Index

Web Sites

Due to the changing nature of Internet links, PowerKids Press has developed an online list of Web sites related to the subject of this book. This site is updated regularly. Please use this link to access the list:

www.powerkidslinks.com/amst/az/